Affirmations
for
Empaths

Affirmations
for
Empaths

A YEAR OF GUIDED JOURNALING

JUDITH ORLOFF, MD

sounds true
BOULDER, COLORADO

Sounds True
Boulder, CO 80306

© 2022 Judith Orloff

Sounds True is a trademark of Sounds True, Inc.

Published 2022

Cover design by Lisa Kerans
Book design by Lisa Kerans and Karen Polaski

The wood used to produce this book is from Forest Stewardship Council (FSC) certified forests, recycled materials, or controlled wood.

Printed in Canada
BK06480
ISBN 978-1-68364-973-1
10 9 8 7 6 5 4 3 2 1

Contents

The Power & Magic of Affirmations

I ADORE AFFIRMATIONS because they are simple, quick, and effective ways to stay in your best self and reframe unproductive thoughts. I use them personally and recommend them to my patients. Affirmations are potent tools that can radically enhance the quality of your life.

I consider affirmations friends whom I can call upon when I need to regain my center, reinforce my strengths, or compassionately adjust my attitude. For empaths and all caring people, they are a crucial element of self-care. Affirmations will help you manage the challenges of being sensitive, such as taking on other people's stress and over-giving, and to embrace the gifts, such as intuition and the joyfulness of connection.

Affirmations are not meant to "emotionally bypass" difficult feelings or sugarcoat hurt with inspiring words. They are positive statements to counter fears, self-doubts, anxieties, and negative stories that replay in your mind. Affirmations help you reprogram outdated beliefs—and they are energy shifters. Words and beliefs contain emotional energy. Affirmations let you say "no"

1

to any thoughts and energies that don't serve you and help you say "yes" to a new mindset.

As a psychiatrist, I know how vital it is to heal emotional wounds with the proper therapeutic support. However, I also realize that much of suffering is amplified by a lack of self-love. Affirmations let you gently shift the beliefs that keep you from lovingly accepting yourself and others.

When you regularly use affirmations, you can replace shame-based notions such as "I'm too sensitive" with "I am proud of my empathy." This kind of deceptively simple turnabout in how you view yourself can liberate positive energy and relieve tension you may not even realize that you had.

This book's central message is: "You are an empathic, talented person. You are 'enough' right now, and always have been." Still, be prepared: A critical voice within will be quick to argue and offer a string of examples to inflame your self-doubts. You might ask this voice, "Really? Will I ever be enough?" Its ultimate answer, no matter how many "improvements" it suggests, is "never." I profoundly reject this notion. I hope you do, too.

I invite you to set aside all the disempowering stories others have told you about yourself and commit to solidifying your own authentic voice. Of course, in life you'll have healing challenges of all shapes and sizes, but you are whole and courageous enough to handle them. Let these affirmations strengthen this knowing.

Really? [handwritten margin note]

You can apply affirmations in different ways.

- To reinforce a positive belief you already possess
- To solidify a shaky belief or behavior
- To create an entirely new belief that you don't have yet but long to make your own

If an affirmation is currently more of a goal than where you are actually at now, repeat it anyway. Think of this stage of change as a rehearsal. Sometimes "acting as if" sets more productive patterns into action. For instance, you can affirm "I am enough" or "It is not healthy to take on other people's suffering" even though you might not fully believe it yet. Your willingness to change is sufficient to set the power of the affirmation in motion.

A key to an affirmation's success is repetition—this moves a belief from your conscious to your subconscious mind. If you keep hearing a message, it's more likely to sink in. Repetition lets you practice a skill so it becomes easier. When you stop reinforcing dysfunctional habits, updated healthy ones can replace them.

HOW TO USE THIS BOOK

Follow these steps to use this journal as a yearlong course to ignite your personal transformation through affirmation:

1. Focus on one affirmation per week
This gives you the luxury of unrushed time each week to practice the principle, invite it into your being, and notice your resistances and breakthroughs. The beauty of having a week devoted

to each affirmation for a year is that you can immerse yourself in its meaning and apply it to your life.

2. Read in any order

You can start at the beginning of the book and proceed in sequence throughout the year. Or you can begin with any of the eight topic areas that you most resonate with and choose your own order. Sometimes you may want to intuitively turn to a random page to find that day's perfect affirmation for you.

3. Repeat the affirmation daily

In a relaxed state, slowly repeat the affirmation inwardly or aloud at least three times in one sitting, and as many times throughout the day as you like. Let go. Come from your heart. There is no need to overthink or effort. The more at ease you are, the more the affirmation can work its magic.

As part of your routine, I recommend saying the affirmation when you first wake up, which sets an inspiring tone every morning, and then again before bedtime, which prepares your unconscious to process the new thought pattern or behavior during sleep.

Some of my patients like to chant the affirmation as a mantra, which is a repetitive sacred sound, song, or utterance, as a creative way to connect with the change they desire. Similarly, you can utilize affirmations both as a mental discipline and also as a ritual invoking a deeper impulse within to change.

4. Journal on the affirmations

In the journaling pages following each of the fifty-two affirmations, I have provided three questions to help you clarify your goals. They are:

- Why is this affirmation important to me?
- What beliefs do I need to release to live this principle fully?
- As a sensitive person, how can my life specifically benefit from making this shift?

In addition, feel free to write about any insights that arise from the topic and the shift in mindset you wish to achieve. Feel free to draw or doodle your realizations, too. Do they have a color or shape? Be open. Try not to censor or edit what emerges.

Throughout the year, you can revisit what you've written about any affirmation in the book if you want to refresh your connection to it.

5. Access the power of your intuition

It can also be illuminating and fun to pull a card each week from a deck such as one I created, *The Empath's Empowerment Deck: 52 Cards to Guide and Inspire Sensitive People*, or your favorite oracle deck. See what synchronicities arise. Working with a card plus an affirmation is a magical formula for change.

Over the next year, let *Affirmations for Empaths* be your personal diary and safe place to return to when you want to be uplifted, supported, and transformed. Let it help you find yourself again, whatever you're facing. Let your practice nurture your highest self, your empathy, and the light within.

The path of affirmations is fun, true, and friendly. The time has come to retire all those reasons why not to love, honor, and cherish yourself. So make a bow, take a breath, and say goodbye to the relics of those old beliefs. Keep moving forward to the freedom and self-worth that awaits you when you value your sensitive nature. Know that you are right where you are supposed to be, and all is well. Get ready. Here comes the Sun.

Judith Orloff, MD
Venice Beach, California

PART
ONE

Treasuring
Yourself

I am a
warrior empath.
I am a kind,
strong, and
loving person.

Why is this affirmation
important to me?

What beliefs do I need to release
to live this principle fully?

As a sensitive person, how can my life
specifically benefit from making this shift?

When I honor
my sensitivities
and practice
daily self-care,
I feel balanced
and serene.

Why is this affirmation important to me?

What beliefs do I need to release
to live this principle fully?

As a sensitive person, how can my life specifically benefit from making this shift?

As I grow
as an empath,
I treat myself
with a little more
kindness every day.
I am enough
right now and
I always have been.

Why is this affirmation
important to me?

What beliefs do I need to release
to live this principle fully?

As a sensitive person, how can my life specifically benefit from making this shift?

I choose to focus on
what's right in my
life and all that is
positive within me.
I cherish myself
and the gift
of being alive.

Why is this affirmation important to me?

What beliefs do I need to release to live this principle fully?

As a sensitive person, how can my life
specifically benefit from making this shift?

My inner child
is magical!
We find time
to take a break
for fun and
play together.

Why is this affirmation important to me?

What beliefs do I need to release
to live this principle fully?

As a sensitive person, how can my life
specifically benefit from making this shift?

PART TWO

Nurturing
Vitality

I tune in to my
energy level
throughout the day.
I know how I am
feeling and respect
my body's needs.

Why is this affirmation important to me?

What beliefs do I need to release
to live this principle fully?

As a sensitive person, how can my life
specifically benefit from making this shift?

I feel energized when I decide to be around positive people. I find kind but firm ways to limit my exposure to draining people.

Why is this affirmation
important to me?

What beliefs do I need to release
to live this principle fully?

As a sensitive person, how can my life
specifically benefit from making this shift?

My life is balanced.
I intentionally
move at a
comfortable pace.
There is no
need to rush or
overschedule.

Why is this affirmation important to me?

What beliefs do I need to release
to live this principle fully?

As a sensitive person, how can my life specifically benefit from making this shift?

I am responsible
only for my own
energy. I am able
to observe the
energy of others
without taking on
their stress.

Why is this affirmation
important to me?

What beliefs do I need to release to live this principle fully?

As a sensitive person, how can my life
specifically benefit from making this shift?

Sleep is my friend.
I treasure the
rest time that
brings me calm
and well-being.

Why is this affirmation
important to me?

What beliefs do I need to release
to live this principle fully?

As a sensitive person, how can my life
specifically benefit from making this shift?

I empower myself
as an empath
every time
I decrease
stimulation in
the face of
sensory overload.

Why is this affirmation important to me?

What beliefs do I need to release
to live this principle fully?

As a sensitive person, how can my life
specifically benefit from making this shift?

Creating Wellness

My natural empathy
makes my body,
mind, and spirit
strong and resilient.

Why is this affirmation
important to me?

What beliefs do I need to release
to live this principle fully?

As a sensitive person, how can my life
specifically benefit from making this shift?

I treat my body
with compassion.
It knows how
to heal swiftly
and with ease.

Why is this affirmation important to me?

What beliefs do I need to release
to live this principle fully?

As a sensitive person, how can my life specifically benefit from making this shift?

I feel centered
when I have
adequate downtime
to process the
events of the day.

Why is this affirmation important to me?

What beliefs do I need to release
to live this principle fully?

As a sensitive person, how can my life
specifically benefit from making this shift?

As I breathe stress
out of my body,
I feel my life force
growing stronger.

Why is this affirmation important to me?

What beliefs do I need to release
to live this principle fully?

As a sensitive person, how can my life specifically benefit from making this shift?

I feel happy
and relaxed
when I let myself
laugh and be
lighthearted.

Why is this affirmation
important to me?

What beliefs do I need to release to live this principle fully?

As a sensitive person, how can my life
specifically benefit from making this shift?

PART FOUR

Balancing Emotions

I learn from the challenges of adversity to be especially tender and compassionate with myself during stressful times.

Why is this affirmation
important to me?

What beliefs do I need to release
to live this principle fully?

As a sensitive person, how can my life
specifically benefit from making this shift?

Whatever the
situation, I know
I can rely on my
inner guidance
to find the
best solution.

Why is this affirmation
important to me?

What beliefs do I need to release
to live this principle fully?

As a sensitive person, how can my life
specifically benefit from making this shift?

I am able
to identify
my emotional
triggers and
compassionately
begin to heal them.

Why is this affirmation important to me?

What beliefs do I need to release
to live this principle fully?

As a sensitive person, how can my life
specifically benefit from making this shift?

Since I often feel
things strongly,
I create quietude
in my life to
balance the
intensity with calm.

Why is this affirmation important to me?

What beliefs do I need to release
to live this principle fully?

As a sensitive person, how can my life specifically benefit from making this shift?

I focus on what
I am grateful
for rather than
obsessing about my
"to-do" list, problems,
or the future.

Why is this affirmation important to me?

What beliefs do I need to release to live this principle fully?

As a sensitive person, how can my life
specifically benefit from making this shift?

Today I make
a commitment
to lead a life
based on love,
not fear.

Why is this affirmation
important to me?

What beliefs do I need to release
to live this principle fully?

As a sensitive person, how can my life specifically benefit from making this shift?

Building
Healthy
Relationships

I deserve to have
caring relationships
with people
who respect
my sensitivities.

Why is this affirmation important to me?

What beliefs do I need to release
to live this principle fully?

As a sensitive person, how can my life
specifically benefit from making this shift?

Knowing that
I don't have to be
constantly on call
for friends in need
is a form of
self-care.

Why is this affirmation
important to me?

What beliefs do I need to release
to live this principle fully?

As a sensitive person, how can my life
specifically benefit from making this shift?

I can express
empathy for a
loved one or
colleague without
taking on their
stress or trying
to fix them.

Why is this affirmation important to me?

What beliefs do I need to release
to live this principle fully?

116

As a sensitive person, how can my life specifically benefit from making this shift?

I protect my
energy and set
a healthy boundary
by saying a loving
"no" to a request.

Why is this affirmation important to me?

What beliefs do I need to release
to live this principle fully?

120

As a sensitive person, how can my life
specifically benefit from making this shift?

I balance my need
to over-help
or micromanage
someone's behavior
by allowing them
the dignity of
their own path.

Why is this affirmation
important to me?

What beliefs do I need to release
to live this principle fully?

124

As a sensitive person, how can my life
specifically benefit from making this shift?

I am accountable
for my own
choices and actions.
I am clear, intuitive,
and purposeful.

Why is this affirmation important to me?

What beliefs do I need to release
to live this principle fully?

128

As a sensitive person, how can my life
specifically benefit from making this shift?

I grow emotionally
as I let resentments
go and become free
from the residue
of past hurts.

Why is this affirmation
important to me?

What beliefs do I need to release
to live this principle fully?

As a sensitive person, how can my life specifically benefit from making this shift?

I value supportive
relationships and
seek exposure
to non-toxic and
low-drama people.

Why is this affirmation
important to me?

What beliefs do I need to release
to live this principle fully?

As a sensitive person, how can my life specifically benefit from making this shift?

As a balanced empath, I allow myself to receive support from people, even if giving feels more natural.

Why is this affirmation important to me?

What beliefs do I need to release
to live this principle fully?

As a sensitive person, how can my life
specifically benefit from making this shift?

When I value my own needs rather than overly focusing on the problems of others, I am deepening my commitment to self-care.

Why is this affirmation
important to me?

What beliefs do I need to release
to live this principle fully?

As a sensitive person, how can my life
specifically benefit from making this shift?

I don't have to
be a people pleaser
to get others
to like me.

Why is this affirmation important to me?

What beliefs do I need to release
to live this principle fully?

As a sensitive person, how can my life
specifically benefit from making this shift?

I can keep
my center
in stressful
interactions
when I choose
to be patient
and tolerant.

Why is this affirmation important to me?

What beliefs do I need to release
to live this principle fully?

As a sensitive person, how can my life
specifically benefit from making this shift?

Discovering Purpose & Work

As I pause to
reflect on what
brings me passion
and purpose, I begin
to manifest these
insights in my life.

Why is this affirmation
important to me?

What beliefs do I need to release
to live this principle fully?

As a sensitive person, how can my life specifically benefit from making this shift?

I practice love
and service in
whatever work
I choose.

Why is this affirmation important to me?

What beliefs do I need to release
to live this principle fully?

As a sensitive person, how can my life
specifically benefit from making this shift?

I take minibreaks
to decompress
and rejuvenate
myself throughout
the day.

Why is this affirmation
important to me?

What beliefs do I need to release
to live this principle fully?

As a sensitive person, how can my life
specifically benefit from making this shift?

I do what's
possible to make
a goal happen,
then surrender the
results to Spirit
to work its magic
in my life.

Why is this affirmation
important to me?

What beliefs do I need to release
to live this principle fully?

As a sensitive person, how can my life
specifically benefit from making this shift?

I allow for the
natural flow of
life by practicing
patience in
a situation and
letting it unfold.

Why is this affirmation important to me?

What beliefs do I need to release
to live this principle fully?

As a sensitive person, how can my life
specifically benefit from making this shift?

Honoring Intuition

Taking time to
still mental chatter
and listen to
my intuition
lets me make
better decisions.

Why is this affirmation important to me?

What beliefs do I need to release
to live this principle fully?

As a sensitive person, how can my life
specifically benefit from making this shift?

When I trust
my gut feeling
about people and
follow its guidance,
my relationships
get better.

Why is this affirmation important to me?

What beliefs do I need to release
to live this principle fully?

As a sensitive person, how can my life
specifically benefit from making this shift?

No matter what
others may say,
I can trust my
intuition and
what it tells me.

Why is this affirmation
important to me?

What beliefs do I need to release
to live this principle fully?

As a sensitive person, how can my life
specifically benefit from making this shift?

Listening to both
my logical mind
and my intuition
lets me be a
balanced, well-
integrated empath.

Why is this affirmation important to me?

What beliefs do I need to release
to live this principle fully?

As a sensitive person, how can my life
specifically benefit from making this shift?

By staying
in the Now,
I am more present
in my life.

Why is this affirmation
important to me?

What beliefs do I need to release
to live this principle fully?

As a sensitive person, how can my life specifically benefit from making this shift?

Paying attention
to my body's
intuitive signals,
such as pain or
tiredness, is a
powerful way
to support my
well-being.

Why is this affirmation important to me?

What beliefs do I need to release
to live this principle fully?

As a sensitive person, how can my life specifically benefit from making this shift?

Finding
Sanctuary

I connect to
my spirituality
every day by
meditating, walking
in nature, or
simply being still.

Why is this affirmation
important to me?

What beliefs do I need to release
to live this principle fully?

As a sensitive person, how can my life specifically benefit from making this shift?

I am a child of the
Earth, joyfully
in sync with the
natural world and
all its creatures.

Why is this affirmation important to me?

What beliefs do I need to release
to live this principle fully?

As a sensitive person, how can my life
specifically benefit from making this shift?

I feel peaceful
and happy when
I take in the beauty
of the moon and
the night sky.

Why is this affirmation important to me?

What beliefs do I need to release
to live this principle fully?

As a sensitive person, how can my life
specifically benefit from making this shift?

Water helps me
heal and cleanse my
energy, whether
I'm walking by
the ocean or
soaking in a tub.

Why is this affirmation
important to me?

What beliefs do I need to release to live this principle fully?

As a sensitive person, how can my life
specifically benefit from making this shift?

I attune to nature's
vitality and flow
as my body senses
the different
energy and rhythm
of each season.

Why is this affirmation important to me?

What beliefs do I need to release
to live this principle fully?

As a sensitive person, how can my life
specifically benefit from making this shift?

No matter
what I am feeling,
I am not alone.
I am connected
to Spirit and the
collective web of
all living beings.

Why is this affirmation
important to me?

What beliefs do I need to release
to live this principle fully?

As a sensitive person, how can my life specifically benefit from making this shift?

As an empowered
empath, I feel
the wonder and
awe of being alive.
Every moment
is sacred.

Why is this affirmation
important to me?

What beliefs do I need to release
to live this principle fully?

As a sensitive person, how can my life
specifically benefit from making this shift?

Affirmations Index
A Quick Reference Guide

PART THREE **Creating Wellness**

PART SIX **Discovering Purpose & Work**

About the Author

JUDITH ORLOFF, MD, a *New York Times* bestselling author, is a leading voice in the fields of medicine, psychiatry, empathy, and intuitive development. A member of the UCLA Psychiatric Clinical Staff, her bestselling books include *The Empath's Survival Guide*, *Thriving as an Empath*, *Emotional Freedom*, *Positive Energy*, *Guide to Intuitive Healing*, and *Second Sight*. She specializes in treating empaths and sensitive people in her private practice. Find more information about Dr. Orloff's Facebook Empath Support Community and her speaking schedule on her website, drjudithorloff.com.

About Sounds True

SOUNDS TRUE IS a multimedia publisher whose mission is to inspire and support personal transformation and spiritual awakening. Founded in 1985 and located in Boulder, Colorado, we work with many of the leading spiritual teachers, thinkers, healers, and visionary artists of our time. We strive with every title to preserve the essential "living wisdom" of the author or artist. It is our goal to create products that not only provide information to a reader or listener but also embody the quality of a wisdom transmission.

For those seeking genuine transformation, Sounds True is your trusted partner. At SoundsTrue.com you will find a wealth of free resources to support your journey, including exclusive weekly audio interviews, free downloads, interactive learning tools, and other special savings on all our titles.

To learn more, please visit SoundsTrue.com/freegifts or call us toll-free at 800.333.9185.

sounds true
WAKING UP THE WORLD